AF484814

Page 0

Divinely Guided

Faith, Love, Hope, Peace & Joy

Written By:

Linda Diane Lay, Angelia Richhart & Amber Richhart

<u>Books By</u>

Lay Family Publishing

The Essence of a Pearl

The Sugar Orchard

Poetic Colors

Divinely Guided

Faith, Love, Hope, Peace & Joy

Written By

Linda Diane Lay, Angelia Richhart & Amber Richhart

Lay Family Publishing

Title - Divinely Guided: Faith, Love, Hope, Peace & Joy
Copyright © 2016 Lay Family Publishing
Authors: Linda Diane Lay, Angelia Richhart, Amber Richhart, Lay Family &
The Royal House of Normandy Royal Lay Family
All rights reserved. Published in the United States by Lay Family Publishing,
an independent publisher based in Indiana and distributed in paperback in the
United States
Originally published, printed & manufactured in the United States.

No portion of this book may be reproduced in any form without written
permission from the publisher or authors, except as permitted by
U.S. copyright law.

While every precaution has been taken in the preparation of this book,
the publisher assumes no responsibility for errors or omissions, or for damages
resulting from the use of the information contained herein.

Tittle: Divinely Guided: Faith, Love, Hope, Peace & Joy
Authors: Linda Diane Lay, Angelia Richhart, Amber Richhart, Lay Family &
The Royal House of Normandy Royal Lay Family
Description: Christian Living and personal growth based on biblical scriptures.
Identifiers:
(Paperback ISBN:978-1-300-21252-2) (Paperback ISBN: 9798224799404)
(E-book ISBN: 9798201818463) (Hardcover ISBN: 978-1-300-48051-8)
Subjects: Classification BISAC (North America)
REL012070   RELIGION / Christian Living / Personal Growth
REL012040   RELIGION / Christian Living / Inspirational
REL006000   RELIGION / Biblical Studies / General

Lay Family Publishing – Design by Lay Family Publishing
Published & Printed in the United States of America

10   9   8   7   6   5   4   3   2   1

Page 5

Lay Family Publishing

Table of Contents

Divinely Guided 1

Books By 2

Faith...8

Love...24

Hope...36

Peace..49

Joy..60

Prayer of Salvation 70

Scriptures on Faith...................................72

Scriptures on Love...................................73

Scriptures on Hope...................................74

Scriptures on Peace..................................75

Scriptures on Joy 76

Scriptures on Salvation 77

Dedication 78

About the Authors 79

FAITH

Faith

- <u>**Hebrews 11:1**</u>

"Now faith is the substance of things hoped for, the evidence of things not seen."

I wanted to start this book with a scripture about faith because, with faith, all things are possible to those who believe. If you are beginning your walk with Jesus Christ or have been a believer for a long time, this book is to help you learn to lean into God and strengthen your relationship and your faith in him. For we shall all go through many trials in this life, and every new and old believer will have to stand the test of faith more than once in their walk with Jesus Christ. This is what this book is about. I hope you find this book helpful and share it with as many friends and family members as you can, because you never know who may be struggling on their journey in life or just need an uplifting word.

- <u>**Psalm 119:30**</u>

"I have chosen the way of faithfulness. I have set my heart on your laws."

In order for one to have and develop faith, one must have an open heart to be able to accept the unseen and believe in the possibility of all things without a doubt. Every day we open our eyes and begin our day. We always take for granted that when we place our feet on the floor, we will be able to walk. You never question this, due to the simple fact that you have an undeniable foundation that was built on faith and trust. Since you were a child, your legs would carry you and take you wherever you wanted to go.

This is where our journey begins with building a solid foundation on faith by trusting Jesus that no matter what situation we face, Jesus Christ will carry us through the trials and tribulations step by step. If we learn to lean into him every day of our lives and listen to him with our hearts, but first we must learn to walk with him.

<u>**So, what is faith?**</u>

➤ <u>**Complete trust or confidence in someone or something.**</u>

➤ <u>**Believing in something based on spiritual apprehension rather than proof.**</u>

• <u>**Mark 10:52**</u>

"Go," said Jesus, "your faith has healed you." Immediately, he received his sight and followed Jesus along the road.

The man that Mark 10:52 speaks of was completely blind. He couldn't see with his physical eyes, but he had an open heart that was able to receive this miracle. He had learned to trust in what was unseen and learned to trust by faith. His faith in Jesus Christ had made him whole. The man whose name this scripture is about was Bartimaeus, the son of Timaeus. He sat by the roadside begging. I imagine this man had a lot of time to think about the stories people were telling about Jesus. He could have easily dismissed these stories, knowing that he was blind and had never seen proof for himself that Jesus could perform these miracles. Instead of dismissing these stories because he lacked proof, he decided to let the stories of Christ into his heart. Which is what led him to have unfaltering faith in Jesus Christ to heal him. Bartimaeus had cried out for Jesus to heal him. More than once, he was told to hold his peace, but what I love about this man is that he did not let it faze him. He cried that much louder, having faith that Jesus Christ would hear his cry, and Jesus did!

Jesus Christ knows everything we are going through, from our pains, our struggles, and our hardships, and he knows our hearts. Maybe you picked this book up randomly, but this book was meant for you. No one ever said that this would be easy and that our path would be smooth sailing. If it were easy, why would you need faith? Having faith means having confidence in what we hope for and the assurance that Jesus Christ will work it out, no matter the situation. Once you develop full faith in him, you will be able to put full trust in him and be able to withstand any storm that you will encounter. True faith is knowing without a doubt that Jesus Christ is the son of God who went to the cross, died for you, and rose again on the third day. He took all your sins so you could receive his eternal gift of salvation.

- <u>**John 3:16**</u>

"God so loved the world that he gave his one and only Son, that whoever believes in him shall not perish but have everlasting life."

- <u>**Jeremiah 1:5**</u>

"Before I formed you in the womb, I knew you; before you were born, I set you apart." "I appointed you as a prophet to the nations."

<u>**Yes, Jesus Christ loves you that much! Because he already knows you!**</u>

Our faith will be tested many times as new believers or as seasoned believers. We must always remember that Jesus wants the best for you.

- **<u>Jeremiah 29:11</u>**

"For I know the plans I have for you," declares the Lord, "plans to prosper you and not to harm you, plans to give you hope and a future."

God wants you to be happy, to have a future, and to love and be loved. He wants you to have all this, and he will give you these things and more if you follow him with all your heart and put him first in your life. A lot of Christians ask God in prayer for things they want or things that they believe will make them happy, and they are upset when they think that their prayers are not heard or that they didn't receive what they asked for. There are many Christians who have encountered this. Christ did hear your prayer, but was it according to his will, and is it for your better good? This goes back to Jeremiah 29:11. He has plans for you—to prosper you and not to harm you.

As you grow as a Christian, your faith in him will strengthen. You will understand that he has your best interests at heart; why wouldn't he? He loves you! If you continue to walk with him, you will come to this understanding. Sometimes you will wonder why something did not work out, or why something failed, or maybe even why certain people are treating you a specific way; the list goes on and on. You may question this over and over in your mind. You must keep your faith, no matter how bleak or negative a situation is or how unfair or unjust something feels. Jesus is right beside you and will work it out for your better good. It may be hard to see or perceive it now, but later in the future you'll be thanking God that what you wanted is not what you got. When enough time passes, you may just be happy that things worked out the way they did. God sees things we cannot see and sees a higher perspective for our better good. We will always go through seasons in life as we age, but we will also go through different seasons in our relationship with Jesus Christ. We will be tested, and we will be tried.

We encounter these things as we mature as Christians: Do you praise God when he blesses you? Will you praise God when you are in the valley or when your circumstances look bleak? These are the things that define us as Christians, if you can praise God through the storms, and do you praise him or remember him when your life isn't picture perfect.

- ### Job 1:20-21

20. At this, Job got up and tore his robe and shaved his head. Then he fell to the ground in worship 21. And said, "Naked I came from my mother's womb, and naked I will depart." "The Lord gave, and the Lord has taken away." "May the name of the Lord be praised."

Job was a wealthy man in the Bible; he was tested and tried for his faith. He lost everything, from his wealth to his kids to his wife, but remained faithful to God. We live in an imperfect world where sin thrives, and the devil is always trying to steal our faith, hope, joy, peace, and belief in Jesus Christ. He will use every worldly measure to do it. We have to remember that Jesus Christ has placed each one of us here for his specific will and not let anyone keep you from God's will in your life. A lot of new believers will always ask the question, why do bad things happen to good people? My answer is pretty simple: we live in a sinful world where nothing is perfect and where the adversary, the devil, tries to steal your belief in God, your happiness, your joy, and everything that is good. Even though we may be tested, just remember.

- **<u>James 1:2-3</u>**

2. "Consider it pure joy, my brothers and sisters, whenever you face trials of many kinds." 3. "Because you know that the testing of your faith produces perseverance."

Therefore, I believe having a deep-rooted faith in Jesus Christ, is the beginning of developing a relationship with him that can't be moved. Jesus never forgets us; the only thing he forgets is our sins. It seems that life has a way of pulling us away from him. Especially now since there are so many things to keep us occupied with social media and life's daily struggles. We make time for the things that we want; don't let your relationship with Jesus Christ fall to the wayside. Make him your priority because he has already made you his.

- <u>Mathew 13:1-11</u>

1. That same day, Jesus went out of the house and sat by the lake. 2. Such large crowds gathered around him that he got into a boat and sat in it, while all the people stood on the shore. 3. Then he told them about many things in parables, saying, "A farmer went out to sow his seed." 4. "As he was scattering the seed, some fell along the path, and the birds came and ate it up." 5. "Some fell on rocky places where it did not have much soil. It sprang up quickly because the soil was shallow." 6. "But when the sun came up, the plants were scorched, and they withered because they had no root." 7. "Other seed fell among thorns, which grew up and choked the plants." 8. "Still other seed fell on good soil, where it produced a crop a hundred, sixty, or thirty times what was sown." 9. "Whoever has ears, let them hear." 10. The disciples came to him and asked, "Why do you speak to the people in parables?" 11. He replied, "Because the knowledge of the secrets of the kingdom of heaven has been given to you, but not to them."

<u>If you keep reading Matthew 13:18–23, it continues to reveal the parables to you.</u>

- <u>**Matthew 13:18–23**</u>

18. Listen then to what the parable of the Sower means: 19. "When anyone hears the message about the kingdom and does not understand it, the evil one comes and snatches away what was sown in their heart." "This is the seed sown along the path." 20. "The seed falling on rocky ground refers to someone who hears the word and at once receives it with joy." 21. "But since they have no roots, they last only a short time. When trouble or persecution comes because of the word, they quickly fall away." 22. "The seed falling among the thorns refers to someone who hears the word, but the worries of this life and the deceitfulness of wealth chokes the word, making it unfruitful." 23. "But the seed falling on good soil refers to someone who hears the word and understands it. This is the one who produces a crop, yielding a hundred, sixty, or thirty times what was sown."

When your relationship with Jesus Christ starts, this is when your life really begins. When your faith in Jesus Christ has matured, you know without a doubt that he is your lord and savior who died for you. You will also know that he took all your sins and washed them away. If someone were to ask me what true love is, I would tell them that true love is the love of Jesus Christ. His love can move mountains, and it's a love that can change your life, an unconditional love that can never be matched, and a love that always stands the test of time. His love is a pillar of strength in my life. Put your faith in Jesus Christ and do not put your faith in man or this world. People in this world will always let you down or disappoint you, no matter if you have been friends for years. People are people, and we cannot always expect them to be there for us, or to want the same things as us, or to see everything the same way.

Everyone on earth will either hurt you or let you down. There will never be anyone here who will never hurt your feelings, so love them. Just try to understand that people are never perfect, no matter who they are. Some people are so broken and hurt that they believe if they find someone who loves them, it can fix their entire life or make them whole again. Or they believe it can fill this void in themselves. People crave an unconditional love that goes beyond words. They crave a love that they believe will fill their lives, or a love that completes them where they feel that they are accepted. Therefore, this is why so many times we find ourselves let down and disappointed in life. We are always searching for perfection or the approval of others in everything we do because so many of us are looking towards worldly things to fill this void or expecting people to love us as Christ loves us.

Once you have fixed your eyes on Jesus, you will no longer need people's approval or the world's approval of you. You only need him. You may lose some people along the way when you start following Jesus Christ, but the people that you lose were not supposed to be in your life anyhow. If you follow the path that God has laid out for you in your heart, you will never be alone, and you are complete in him.

- **<u>1 John 5:4</u>**

"For everyone born of God overcomes the world." "This is the victory that has overcome the world and even our faith."

- **<u>Philippians 4:13</u>**

"I can do all this through him, who gives me strength."

- **<u>Colossians 2:10</u>**

"And you are complete in Him, who is the head of all principality and power."

Faith is the inner understanding that even when your life is upside down and nothing is going right, Jesus Christ is there for you. He will lead you step by step out of the valley, no matter how difficult the situation is. Faith operates in the unseen and is deeply rooted in love. Faith is also knowing that Jesus loves you and that you are never alone.

Even if you feel unworthy, not good enough, or like you cannot be forgiven, or like you keep making the wrong decisions, or maybe you feel as if God has forgotten about you, faith is knowing that you are so loved by God that he will never leave you, never abandon you, and never forsake you. He loves you so much that he gave his life for you. Do not let the devil speak lies to you and cause you to stumble by tellIng you lies such as you'll never be good enough, or it's too late for you, or God doesn't love you. Take a step of faith and say to yourself that God loves me!

- <u>Isaiah 49:16</u>

"See, I have engraved you on the palms of my hands; your walls are ever before me."

- <u>John 10:28</u>

"I give them eternal life, and they shall never perish; no one will snatch them out of my hand."

- <u>Isaiah 49:15</u>

"Can a woman forget her nursing child that she should have no compassion for the son of her womb?" "Surely, they may forget, yet I will not forget you."

LOVE

Love

Love encompasses a range of strong emotions and positive emotional and mental states. Love is the most sublime virtue and good habit, from the deepest interpersonal affection to the simplest pleasures. So, what is love? So, understanding love from a written description would be a little difficult to understand unless, of course, you've experienced love in its many forms. I believe that love in all its facets is uniquely beautiful and is a large part of our lives because it's human nature to love and want to be loved and accepted.

God's love for us is a divine love, an all-encompassing unconditional love that is fulfilling to the inner depths of our hearts. No matter how far you stray from God, he's always there, waiting for you with open arms to come back. He fully accepts you just the way you are no matter how many sins you have or how flawed you feel, Jesus is always willing to forgive and accept you back. You are a very loved child of God, so loved that he died for you and gave up his life willingly to save you.

- ## John 3:16

"For God so loved the world that he gave his only begotten Son, that whosoever believeth in him should not perish but have everlasting life."

- ## 1 John 4:16

"And so, we know and rely on the love God has for us. God is love." "Whoever lives in love lives in God, and God in them."

To know Jesus Christ is to know true love. The more you open your heart to him, the more you'll know him and what true love is. Like a mother who loves her children, she never wants to see anything bad happen to them, and she never wants to see them go through hardships or trouble in their lives.

No mother wants this for her children, but if her children do go through these things, she will always be there to help them. She will console them or give them the wisdom or advice they need in their situation. She has an unmatched, unconditional love for her children and would even give up her life to save them. So, this is the same with Jesus Christ. Jesus

Christ gave up his life because he loved you. He loves you unconditionally and is always there for you to lean on when life's burdens become too much. He's not the cause of your problems, but he is always there trying to lead you through your problems. Maybe you blame God for the way your life is, or how it turned out, or why something happened, but Christ isn't to blame; he only came to save you.

Love is always freely given and freely received. Jesus won't force you to love him, even though he loves you unconditionally. There is nothing you can do that can make him not love you. You are a child of Almighty God! Like I stated earlier, you can never force love; it is freely given and freely received. If you force love, it will always lead to resentment. This is why he gave us free will. He wants you to love him and have a relationship with him, but he won't force you to love him or follow him.

It's the same with an adult who would choose to disown or not associate with a parent. The parent would still love their child unconditionally, but there's not much a parent can do to get their child to understand that they love them. It's up to the individual to want to accept their love and have a relationship with them. You can't blame God for all the woes in your world and all the troubles you will encounter. Suffering is caused by sin, whether it's your sin or someone else's, and we all suffer bad things sometimes.

There's evil in this world. So don't let your heart be burdened by holding onto anger, resentment, or a grudge against God for what someone has done to you or why something in your life didn't work out like you had planned or had hope for. I believe that when we get rejected by either people or any other circumstance in our lives, the rejection is God's protection. If you put all your love and faith in Jesus Christ and trust him, he will show you the plans he has for you and your life. Jesus can open doors no man can and make things in your life happen you never thought were possible.

- **<u>Psalm 139: 1-4</u>**

1. "You have searched me, Lord, and you know me." 2. "You know when I sit and when I rise; you perceive my thoughts from afar." 3. "You discern my going out and my lying down; you are familiar with all my ways." 4. "Before a word is on my tongue, you, Lord, know it completely."

- **<u>Matthew 19:26</u>**

But Jesus looked at them and said, "With man, this is impossible, but with God, all things are possible."

If you can't love yourself, you will never be able to love anyone. If you hate yourself, all those things will boil to the surface and reflect on everyone you know. This is why forgiveness and love are so important. Remember, everyone's different, and we are all made in the image of God uniquely, meaning there is only one of you. You are very special to Christ, which is why he created you.

- **<u>Song of Songs 4:7</u>**

"You are altogether beautiful, my darling. There is no flaw in you."

- **<u>1 Peter 4:8</u>**

"Above all, love each other deeply, because love covers a multitude of sins.'

When you start leading a godly life and you live for God and not for this world, you are going to be met with opposition. You could end up losing good friends, or your family may not support you. You may even feel as if your life is crumbling. You just must remember that God is bigger than all your problems, and he will walk you through them step by step. The adversary hates you and hates that you are shining God's light and love, and he will always try to make you stumble. Maybe the adversary told you that you were not good enough, that no one could ever love you, or that Jesus could never forgive you. Maybe he even tried to tell you it's too late to change your life, or that you'll never get well, or any other lie, but that's exactly what they are: lies.

The devil will try to get you to blame your family, Jesus, or anyone else for your problems or why your life is like it is. The devil wants you to be offended and mad at God and everyone else for your problems. He only does this to try to pull you away from the love of Christ and to try to make you fall away from the plans God has for you. He will also try to separate you or create wedges with you and your family, or blockages or strongholds between you and them. If the devil can create strife, it will lead to anger, resentment, grief, bitterness, loneliness, depression, and so on. If you allow him to do this, it can tear your life and your relationships apart. So don't let the devil plant seeds of hate in your life. The devil wants you to be bitter, depressed, lonely, miserable, or worried all the time.

He loves it when people argue or say hurtful things to each other or even when you tear yourself down so much to the point you lose your own faith in yourself or your own self-worth. When you become hurt, offended, and angry, you'll end up hurting others emotionally. It's a vicious cycle that only stops when we grow as Christians, quit holding onto grudges and anger, and refuse to fall into the devil's traps. Perhaps you suffered an injustice, or something didn't work out the way you planned, but God will see you through it and lead you through it with his provision, strength, and love. You may not understand why this happened or even question it, but God will always use what the devil meant to harm you for your better good. God will always give you the wisdom, courage, and strength to overcome your problems. Maybe you went through something hard so that you could possibly help others who are going through something similar, and the more opposition and hardships you go through, the stronger you become.

- **<u>Deuteronomy 31:6</u>**

"Be strong and courageous." "Do not be afraid or terrified because of them, for the Lord your God goes with you; he will never leave you nor forsake you."

- **<u>Isaiah-41:10</u>**

"So do not fear, for I am with you." "Do not be dismayed, for I am your God." "I will strengthen you and help you; I will uphold you with my righteous right hand."

- **<u>Psalm 18:2</u>**

"The Lord is my rock, my fortress, and my deliverer; my God is my rock, in whom I take refuge." "He is my shield and the horn of my salvation, my stronghold."

A lot of people always ask, If God is all love, why wouldn't he make a sinless world? Well, he did, but man brought sin into this world with our fleshy nature. The devil uses temptation to cause us to sin, and when we sin, we sin against ourselves, others, and God. Sin is always accompanied by trouble, grief, or suffering, and it's always caused by our sins or someone else's. We usually feel condemned or guilty when we sin, but this is why we live by faith and grace through Jesus Christ.

You will never be sinless or perfect, no matter how hard you try, but God knows this. This is why Jesus Christ came to die on the cross for us and to save us from our sins, and to him I'm eternally grateful. When you are serious about following Jesus, even if you fall or backslide in your faith, Jesus Christ will always forgive you and accept you back. Your life will drastically change, and he will open doors in your life that no man could've opened. Your life will start reflecting everything that Jesus is, which is love. You will no longer care about worldly things, and these things will all fall away.

- **<u>Corinthians 5:17</u>**

"Therefore, if anyone is in Christ, the new creation has come." **"The old has gone; the new is here!"**

- **<u>Romans 12:2</u>**

"Do not conform to the pattern of this world but be transformed by the renewal of your mind." "Then you will be able to test and approve what God's will is - his good, pleasing, and perfect will."

Your mind and heart will change first in how you think, act, and feel. Then all the subconscious changes in your mind and in your heart will pour out into your flesh and change you as a whole. When you truly follow Jesus Christ, your mind will be renewed, and you will live from glory to glory and from victory to victory. When a gardener has a rose bush, he will always prune away all the old limbs, leaves, and stems, and only the preserves the good. He does this so that the rose will continue to grow and flourish. It will develop deeper roots, more limbs, and more leaves so that it can bloom more beautiful roses. Of course, this takes time, so this is the same for you. God doesn't want you to hold onto all your past hurts, pains, failures, or emotional turmoil you have been taking with you everywhere you go. It only holds you down, and sometimes what life takes us through is hard to handle, hard to cope with, or hard to go through. If you can manage to open your heart to God, even if you've been hurt or are still hurting, God will see to it that you have beautiful roses to show for your pain and for others to appreciate.

- **<u>John 15:1-2</u>**

1. "I am the true vine, and my father is the gardener." 20. "He cuts off every branch in me that bears no fruit, while every branch that does bear fruit, he prunes so that it will be even more fruitful."

HOPE

Hope

Hope is a feeling of expectation and a desire for a certain thing to happen. It is an optimistic state of mind that is based on the expectation of positive outcomes with respect to the events and circumstances in one's life and /or the world at large.

"Expect with confidence."

- **Isaiah 40:31**

"But those who hope in the Lord will renew their strength."
"They will soar on wings like eagles; they will run and not grow weary; they will walk and not be faint."

- **<u>Hebrews 10:23</u>**

"Let us hold unswervingly to the hope we profess, for he who promised is faithful."

Hope is a beautiful thing, and I do believe that there are two types of hope. One is a worldly hope that is wishy-washy, and even though you may have it, there is a place in you that believes it may or may not happen. It is almost as if you hope for the best but do not truly believe the best would be your ultimate outcome in a situation. That is a worldly hope. Hope that comes from Christ or hope that is built on the foundation of the word of God, is always a positive belief in having favorable expectations in your life and your circumstances. It is also a happy anticipation that good things are going to happen, no matter what your circumstances are, and that God will work things out for your better good. A godly hope, or a Christ-like hope, is to simply have a positive attitude and a positive mindset. People hope for things they do not have or are in lack thereof. A lot of times we are hoping with a worldly hope and not putting our faith in our hope to believe God's words and promises. You can choose to have the hope that Christ wants you to possess, and you can choose to be hopeful and always see the positive things in life. It is always your decision; your feelings and emotions are always changing with day-to-day life.

You are the only one who can control your emotions, thoughts, and feelings. Don't keep yourself locked up in a prison because of your circumstances or because of your past negativity or doubt and believe nothing good could happen to you. Choose to believe in God for hope, expect favors in your life, and watch God change your life. Although, you cannot do this with a negative mindset. If you can't believe that your situation is going to change, how much hope and faith do you have in Christ? God is waiting for you to trust him, step out in faith, and put your full hope in him, but first you must capture all the negativity, bad mindsets, and wrong thinking and take them captive and combat all the lies that you believe about yourself and your life. Whether they are lies from the adversary or negative thoughts you made yourself believe over time.

A lot of people lose themselves from being beaten down by the world or people saying negative things to them, like you'll never amount to anything, or your situation will never change. If you allow these thoughts to seep into your mindset, you'll find yourself in depression and despair and could even become hopeless. Being hopeless is either feeling condemned, not good enough, losing your identity, feeling unforgivable, or even feeling like life's not even worth living at its worst.

This is just where the devil wants you—to be trapped in a negative mindset, believing all those lies, and believing that your life will never change. When a person who is encountering a hard situation begins to feel hope, the devil will try to creep in and fight you to steal it. When you feel hopelessness creeping in, stand your ground, know who you are in Christ, and remember all the promises that God will fulfill in your life. Everything in God is good and full of life and hope. It is never too late to begin again. I am not saying your life will be picture perfect and that you will not have bad days if you follow Jesus Christ, but what I am saying is that God died for you to give you life and for you to enjoy it, and to live it in abundance with his word and promises.

- **Psalm 34:18**

"The Lord is close to the brokenhearted and saves those who are crushed in spirit."

- ## <u>Psalm 139:14</u>

"I will praise you, for I am fearfully and wonderfully made." "Marvelous are your works." "And that my soul knows very well."

<u>Fearfully is a Hebrew word meaning "yare," which means to respect, revere, honor, or stand in awe of.</u>

So, when God said that you are fearfully made, he meant that when he made you, you are full of respect, reverence, honor, and awe. You are very special to him, and he does not want to see you in hopelessness, trapped in a dark pit of depression, despair, or worthlessness. He died to give you life, love, and a new beginning. So, believe and be hopeful, and receive it!

- ## <u>Ephesians-1:18</u>

"I pray that the eyes of your heart may be enlightened in order that you may know the hope to which he has called

you, the riches of his glorious inheritance in his holy people."

Sometimes we get so caught up in this world that things lead us to feel completely worthless, unloved, judged, lonely, and sometimes even to the point of self-hatred, or that our lives are completely ruined. Which ultimately leads down a road of despair and illusions. Or maybe you are holding onto too many negative feelings and emotions from your past that are still lingering in your present and disrupting your life. It is hard to have hope if you are constantly dwelling on all the things, you feel that isn't right in your life, or why people have done you a certain way, or if you're just clinging to negativity. Becoming hopeless and dwelling in this pit of darkness usually leads to hatred, whether it is for yourself or others, or self-pity, grief, anger, or even resentment.

In order to change your life, you must change your mind about yourself and refuse to feed the lies the enemy told you. The more you feed something, the more it grows, and perhaps you have been feeding the monster long enough. It is time for you to get freedom and break the chains of bondage the enemy has placed on you. He knows if he can keep you feeling hopeless, worthless, and miserable that he has taken your life hostage and that you won't be able to be any good to yourself, others, or the world. Like I said before, the devil hates you and hates that you are a loved child of Almighty God. He despises you and wants to ruin your life and keep you captive with all the lies he has made you believe, and keep you stuck in a pit of depression, worthlessness, despair, unforgiveness, or even fear.

Forgiveness is a huge milestone when you are trying to escape the pit of hopelessness, because forgiving people for their wrongs against us frees us from the bonds of hate and despair. Maybe you do not feel capable of forgiving someone because they hurt you so badly, but the truth is that you can still forgive them even if you don't feel like it. Maybe what they have done to you has made you feel worthless and hopeless, but by choosing not to forgive, you are choosing to still hold onto all the pain, hurt, and hopelessness you currently have. When we follow Christ, we choose love because it covers a multitude of sins and because you overcome evil with good. When you choose love, you'll come to the understanding that no one is perfect, and that people hurt people. Once you free yourself of the past pain, hurt, and negativity you are holding onto, you'll regain a new perspective on life because you know the things people have done to you don't define you as a person. Then you'll soon regain hope in yourself, your future, and your life.

- **<u>Romans 15:13</u>**

"Now may the God of hope fill you with all joy and peace in believing, that you may abound in hope by the power of the Holy Spirit."

- **<u>Ephesians 4:31-32</u>**

31. "Let all bitterness, and wrath, and anger, and clamor, and evil speaking, be put away from you, with all malice." 32. "And be ye kind one to another, tenderhearted, forgiving one another, even as God, for Christ's sake, has forgiven you."

<u>**God is a restorer, a rebuilder, and a life changer.**</u>

<u>**He gives us hope for a brighter future.**</u>

- <u>**Jeremiah 29:11**</u>

"For I know the plans I have for you, declares the Lord, plans to prosper you and not to harm you, plans to give you hope and a future."

A hopeful person refuses to be negative and always stands in faith, knowing that their hope and their future are good and that all things are possible through God. A hopeful person also refuses to quit or give up; they know that when their hope is in the Lord, there is always a way. God is always right there with you, leading the way.

If you choose to trust Jesus Christ and put your full hope in him, it can change your life dramatically. Even if you have been praying the same prayer for many years, maybe you haven't seen it come to pass. Even though you have been waiting on God. He has not abandoned you, so don't lose your hope. Sometimes we must wait to watch things come together, and maybe your prayers are just around the corner, getting ready to be answered. All good things take time.

- **<u>Matthew 7:11</u>**

"If you, then, though you are evil, know how to give good gifts to your children, how much more will your Father in heaven give good gifts to those who ask him!"

So, keep your hope in God that he will always work out everything for your better good, and knowing that he always has your best interests at heart is the key. Sometimes we may not always get everything we ask for in prayer; there is a valid reason for this. Maybe if your prayer was not answered, it is not because Christ didn't hear you. It's because God knew it wasn't for your better good and that whatever you had asked for would've affected your life in a negative way. God will not hold any good things from you, but he will hold things that are not meant for you. So, keeping your hope and faith in him is truly important because you must trust him and believe in your heart that he has good plans for you and your future. A lot of people lose hope in Christ because they always feel that if Jesus loved me, why wouldn't he answer my prayers? The answer is simple: it was not meant for you, or it is not yet time.

Even though you may not understand this, or maybe you even blame God for not answering your prayers. He has something better in mind for you, and you will eventually come to this understanding in the future when things work out better the way he has them planned. Like a woman who is going through a pregnancy, she wants to rush things along, but she does not know or yet realize that she first needs to be prepared and ready to handle the change and gift that she has been given. Once she realizes this understanding, she will be happy to wait and hope in expectation. You will realize that sometimes God must prepare you first, and he will work things out of you that you're holding onto in your spirit, before he can change you and your life. God cannot give you something in your life if you are not ready or prepared for it. He will not give you something that you are spiritually not able to handle. So be patient; God is working wonders in your lie.

- **James-4:3**

"When you ask, you do not receive, because you ask with wrong motives, that you may spend what you get on your pleasures."

- <u>Psalm 84:11</u>

"For the Lord God is a sun and shield; the Lord will give grace and glory; no good thing will he withhold from them that walk uprightly."

- <u>Psalm 27:14</u>

"Wait on the Lord, be of good courage, and he shall strengthen thine heart. Wait, I say, on the Lord."

PEACE

Peace

Peace is freedom, or a period of freedom from public disturbances or war. It can also be a quiet and calm state of mind, tranquility, or harmony. Peace is classified into two types: internal peace and external peace. Generally speaking. Internal peace is defined as the state of physical and spiritual calm despite many stressors. To find your peace of mind means finding happiness, contentment, and bliss no matter how hard life is or despite what life throws at you. While external peace is peace as the world itself suggests, it is harmony and tranquility in your surroundings, such as your home, your community, etc.

Jesus Christ defines the peace that he was leaving to his disciples and to us as the peace he had himself enjoyed. Peace is a precious gift from God that this world cannot give to you. Jesus gives all his followers his peace, which is an inner peace of heart and soul that only comes through Jesus Christ in the Holy Spirit. A lot of people in this world are constantly up and down in their emotions because they have not realized they're in control of their emotions and don't have to act upon them in a negative way. The other reason why we are unable to be peaceful is because we are always allowing things or circumstances in this world to affect our peace, whether it's an external circumstance or something we have internalized.

In order to be able to live a peaceful life or to have the gift God left us, we must first be able to accept the gift and realize life is never going to be perfect or easy. There will always be people or circumstances that can make you lose your peace. We need to learn to be peacemakers and to not stress so much over our daily lives when circumstances are out of our control. You can go through a really hard time and still be able to keep your peace by choosing to walk in peace. When you choose to walk in peace, there is nothing that can make you upset. To be a peacemaker and to walk in peace means to humble yourself and forgive quickly. I am not saying to keep yourself in a negative situation, but what I am saying is to choose to forgive the people who hurt you and move on with your life, if the situation cannot be mended and pray for them.

By forgiving others, you gift them the gift of forgiveness like Christ gave you, but you also gift yourself the gift of peace. When we become mad, upset, angry, hurt, or even resentful over a situation, we only hurt ourselves and those around us more and more. Some people carry these types of hurts or emotional scars with them for years and refuse to forgive the person who hurt them.

So, they keep the pain in their present time instead of forgiving it and letting it be in the past. While the person who hurt them is out living their life, not even thinking about it. So, what I am saying to you is to choose to have peace and be a peacemaker. God gave you this gift so that you could live your life in peace. Even when we live in peace, there will always be times you may lose your peace by getting upset, getting into an argument, or things not working out for you. When you lose your peace, the most important thing is to remember not to feel guilty or condemned, but to quickly get back to peace. You must always keep still and rest in God.

We are only humans, and we all make mistakes and sin. Our goal as Christians is to be Christ-like in character. Peace is the soul's harmony, and a river of Christ's peace and righteousness lives in you. In order to keep your peace, you cannot do what everybody else does, especially when you don't have peace about it. If your peace is being disturbed, you are sinning against your conscience. Follow peace and whatever gives you peace. Being a peacemaker means that sometimes you hold your tongue in an argument instead of trying to satisfy the flesh by getting the last word. Or even being the first to apologize, even if you do not feel like it. You can never attain peace or God's anointing if you always live in strife.

You must mature as people and as Christians and realize it's not always about getting your way in life. Life is not perfect, and not everything in your life is always going to play out like you expect. But rather, you choose to play the role of a peacemaker in your life, humbling yourself to fix situations, whether it is something you did or did not do, but choosing to do right even if it wasn't your fault. Jesus Christ left his peace with us. Stop permitting yourself to get upset; you have God's gift of peace to make it through any of life's storms.

- <u>**Colossians 3:15**</u>

"Let the peace of Christ rule in your hearts, since, as members of one body, you were called to peace. And be thankful."

- ### <u>Romans 5:1</u>

"Therefore, since we have been justified through faith, we have peace with God through our Lord Jesus Christ."

When you choose to live in peace, you will still encounter different things in life that will test you and try to steal your peace. If you do not feel peaceful about something you have been contemplating doing, like moving or changing jobs, then don't do whatever it is that steals your peace. You will always know when something is right or wrong by either feeling peaceful about the situation or unsettled by it. We should never live our lives constantly with ups and downs emotionally, but we should always surround ourselves with people who are peacemakers and those who follow peace. If strife or arguments do enter your life, confront them as quickly as possible and deal with the matter. A lot of people's troubles in their lives are created by strife, whether it is people saying false rumors or bad things about them, etc. Strife will persist until it wreaks havoc on your life and theirs. Therefore, this is why it's so important when you realize strife is in your life to deal with it and fix the problem. If you are holding onto strife, anger, resentment, or grief, give it to God and forgive the person, your past, or even yourself. Holding onto old wounds, past hurts, and anything else will only steal your anointing and your peace. If you choose to walk in peace, the devil cannot do anything to you because when we walk in peace, Jesus walks with you and will crush the adversary under your feet.

- **<u>Romans 16:20</u>**

"The God of Peace will soon crush Satan under your feet. The grace of our Lord Jesus be with you."

Peace is a place of protection, so wrap yourself in peace, and when you feel turmoil in your life and start getting upset. Stop! Be still, get with God, and learn to be quick to forgive. Do not store up offenses in your heart, for this is the devil's way to lure you into deeper problems and create strife and blockages in your life. Always try to do right and uproot all the seeds of offense, resentment, anger, and grief by learning to forgive yourself and others. We always tend to get hurt or upset when people say things we don't like, and we tend to take it as if they were trying to hurt us or were just being deliberately mean. This is always what causes people to become on guard because they have been hurt before and are still holding onto all the past hurts and emotional scars. You must understand that we are all humans, and we all make mistakes.

Therefore, this is why you can never have a relationship with anyone without forgiveness and love. Every one of us is imperfect, and maybe someone did hurt you, but it could also be because someone hurt them. It is a vicious cycle of hurt and pain, and it's the way the devil works. The devil does not want families, friends, churches, or anyone, for that matter, to get along. All he wants is to bring strife and division into your family, your church, or even your work. He is a peace thief and will do anything to steal your peace and cause strife in your life. What tactics does he use to steal your peace or keep you continuously upset? Refuse to lose your peace and refuse to be intimidated or frightened, no matter what you are facing. Always stand your ground, knowing who you are in Christ. Always remain stable, calm, peaceful, level-minded, and constant, knowing that this is a clear sign to the devil of his impending destruction, and it is also a sign to Jesus Christ that you have the faith and confidence in him for your complete healing and deliverance. By standing in peace and trusting God through your faith, no matter how bleak or helpless your situation may appear, trusting in God and having faith in him is powerful and life changing.

- **Psalm 50:15**

"And call upon me in the day of trouble: I will deliver thee, and thou shalt glorify me."

- **Psalm 107:6**

"Then they cried unto the Lord in their trouble, and he delivered them out of their distress."

- **2 Thessalonians 3:3**

"But the Lord is faithful, and he will strengthen you and protect you from the evil one."

It's not easy until you learn to stay calm in the face of adversity or trouble. This is where your faith comes in; worrying or trying to figure something out only makes you upset and steals your peace and joy. Do not let the devil stir strife in your life and cause disillusions among you, your friends, your family, or in your church. How many times in your life have you gotten worried or upset, and God worked it out and took care of it? The longer you are in a relationship with God and the more you come to know him, the more you will trust him and his word. Whatever you may be going through in your life, just know he will deliver you from it. Always maintain a peaceful, relaxed heart, soul and body, and fight the good fight of faith. You will always have tribulations in this life, but the more that you grow in God, the more spiritual you will become and the stronger you will be. Where unity is, God blesses. God came so that you may enjoy your life and have eternal life in him. Humble yourself and always walk in peace and love, and you will be blessed. You will end up with more than you ever gave up.

- **Matthew 5:9**

"Blessed are the peacemakers, for they will be called children of God."

17. 'But the wisdom that is from above is first pure, then peaceable, gentle, and easy to be intreated, full of mercy and good fruits, without partiality, and without hypocrisy." 18. 'And the fruit of righteousness is sown in the peace of those who make peace."

JOY

Joy

So, joy is a great pleasure and happiness that comes from a sense of well-being. Delight, joyfulness, great pleasure, gladness, jubilee, and/or rejoicing. The joy that comes from Jesus Christ is a joyfulness that makes life worth living in each and every moment because it resonates with our soul's core identity.

We have every reason to be joyful knowing that Christ died for our sins and came to live in our hearts.

- **1 Peter 1:8–9**

8. "Though you have not seen him, you love him, and even though you do not see him now, you believe in him and are filled with an inexpressible and glorious joy." 9. "For you are

receiving the end result of your faith, the salvation of your souls."

- <u>John 16:24</u>

"Until now, you have not asked for anything in my name." "Ask, and you will receive, and your joy will be complete."

So, there is also the type of joy that comes from the world when we are either gifted with something nice or have reached a goal that we have set in our lives. This is a good type of joy to have, but it only lasts for a short while and cannot keep you constantly joyful throughout your life.

We will never live every moment of our lives on the mountaintop; most of our lives are ordinary and sometimes even routine, but you can enjoy your life with God's help to enjoy everything we do. The joy that comes from God is peaceful, uplifting, and even healing. It is a joy that resonates from the inside, knowing that Christ died for you, and if you know and love Jesus, you have this type of joy. It is a fruit of the spirit, and only real joy comes from God and is ours forever. It transforms and regenerates us. Joy in Jesus Christ is an attitude of the heart determined by our confidence in God. It is also a gift of the spirit to have a strong and intimate relationship with Christ, and to truly know Christ is to truly know joy.

- **<u>John 15:11</u>**

"These things have I spoken to you: that my joy might remain in you and that your joy might be full."

- **<u>Psalm 16:11</u>**

"You will show me the path of life." "In Your presence is fullness of joy; at your right hand are pleasures forevermore."

To have hope and faith in Jesus Christ always releases joy because you have a good expectation that something good is going to happen in your life. Sometimes, as Christians, we never experience the fullness of joy that God intended. This is usually because we are letting things in life steal our joy or because we are always worried or even feel guilty for taking the time to enjoy our lives. Maybe it is because you are overstressed or overworked, and you feel like you cannot take a break or that you should not enjoy yourself. Maybe because you feel like if you do, you will fall behind because there is so much that must be done. You are not meant or built to just work, work, work. Even if you just allow yourself to sit and stop and refresh and restore your peace and joy, you will experience more happiness in your life. A lot of times we cannot enjoy our lives because of our mindsets or the perspective that we have chosen, and it could be that you experienced so many bad things that you lost all hope and don't expect anything good to happen to you.

- **Proverbs 23:7**

"For as he thinketh in his heart, so is he."

So, if you are always thinking the worst and never believing anything good could happen, you are letting the devil steal the gifts that God has given you. Which is the gift of hope and joy. We are supposed to rejoice and believe that we will see the goodness and glory of God in our lives. Do not give up on your dreams, yourself, or your family. God can work wonders and miracles in your life. Always be full of joy, even though our lives are not perfect, and rejoice in your troubles because you know that God is going to turn them around and use them for the better good in your life. All things work together for good for those who love Christ.

- <u>**John 10:10**</u>

"The thief comes only to steal and kill and destroy; I have come that they may have life and have it to the full."

- <u>**James 1: 2-3**</u>

2. "Consider it pure joy, my brothers and sisters, whenever you face trials of many kinds," 3. "because you know that the testing of your faith produces perseverance."

You must learn to abide and rest in God. You cannot have enjoyment if you cannot learn to rest in God. By resting in God, this allows you to receive and rejuvenate the peace and joy in your life. Sometimes we cannot enjoy our lives because, even though we have forgiven others and know that God has forgiven us, we still have not forgiven ourselves. We cannot receive God's mercy if we have not forgiven ourselves. God's mercy is God being good to us even though we do not deserve it sometimes. This is usually because some people are not good at receiving because they do not know how to receive. Or they just feel that they are undeserving. This is why Jesus Christ went to the cross for you; he forgave you, and it is time that you forgive yourself and receive the mercy and joy he has for you. You have learned to forgive others; now it is time that you learn to forgive yourself.

- <u>**Romans 8:1**</u>

"There is therefore now no condemnation to those who are in Christ Jesus, who do not walk according to the flesh but according to the Spirit."

- ## 1 John 1:9

"If we confess our sins, He is faithful and just to forgive us our sins and to cleanse us from all unrighteousness."

- ## 1 Peter 5:7

"Casting all your care upon him, for he careth for you."

If you have children or loved ones, it gives you joy to see them enjoying their lives. So how much more does Jesus Christ love seeing us happy and not stressing over our lives worries or feeling condemned all the time? God wants us to experience his love and joy in our everyday lives. We cannot blame others because we are not happy, and we cannot hold others responsible for our joy and happiness in life. Do not let the devil lie to you and steal the joy that God has given you. Cast down all the negativity in your life and in your thoughts and start living a more positive life with peace and joy-filled thoughts. For what a man thinks about, so is he. If you believe you cannot enjoy your life you won't, but that is a thought with wrong thinking and a negative mindset. The Bible even tells you to think of all things good, pure, and holy.

- **<u>Proverbs 17:22</u>**

"A cheerful heart is good medicine. But a crushed spirit dries up the bones."

- **<u>Philippians 4:8</u>**

"Finally, brethren, whatsoever things are true, whatsoever things are honest, whatsoever things are just, whatsoever things are pure, whatsoever things are lovely, whatsoever things are of good report; if there be any virtue, and if there be any praise, think on these things."

So, keep your heart full of love; where love abides, joy grows. The fullness of Christ lies there within. Christ is all love, peace, joy, and hope. He is all things good and holy; he died to give you joy and a future. To give you hope and to give you your life in the fullness of love within him. Do not live with negativity, depression, pain, suffering, or resentment. He died and was resurrected, so your old life has also passed away. The new life that you have is a new creation in him. Full of all life's most precious gifts: love, joy, peace, and true happiness.

Be thankful that he took all our sins from us and took them to the cross. Enjoy your life with him; he will always be there for you and never abandon you. The eternal gift of salvation we receive from him should be enough for you to live a joyful life. Knowing that the Son of God went through all these things and suffering that we encounter here and chose to give up his life because he loves you that much! The only thing that Jesus Christ wants from you is for you to accept him as your Lord and Savior.

- **<u>Matthew 11:28</u>**

"Come to me, all you who are weary and burdened, and I will give you rest."

PRAYER ON SALVATION

Prayer of Salvation

If you have yet to make Jesus Christ the Lord and Savior of your life, we invite you to pray this prayer of salvation.

I come to you in prayer, Lord Jesus Christ, asking for forgiveness of my sins. I confess with my mouth and believe in my heart that Jesus Christ is the son of God and that he died on the cross for me so that my sins may be forgiven, and I may have eternal life. I believe Jesus Christ rose from the grave on the third day, and I ask him to come into my life and into my heart and become my Lord and Savior.

In Jesus Christ's name, we pray.

Amen.

If you prayed that prayer of salvation and truly meant it, we believe that you are saved and are born-again Christian.

Scriptures on Faith

John 3:16

Mark 10:52

John 6:35

Hebrews 11:11

Romans 10:10

1 Corinthians 16:13

Romans 1:17

Galatians 3:26-27

Mark 11-24

Ephesians 3:16-11

Hebrews 11:1

Proverbs 3:5-6

2 Corinthians 5:7

James1:6

Hebrews 11:6

John 11:40

Mark 9:23

Scriptures on Love

1 Corinthians 16:14

Psalm 143:8

Colossians 3:14

Proverbs 3:3-4

1 John 4:16

1 John 4:19

Ephesians 4:2

1 Corinthians 13:13

1 Peter 4:8

Romans 12:14

1 Corinthians 13:2

John 15:12

Isaiah 49:15-16

Romans 12:10

Ephesians 5:25-26

John 15:13

1 Corinthians 2:9

Scriptures on Hope

Jeremiah 29:11

Isaiah 40:31

Psalm 121:7-8

Romans 15:13

Matthew 11:28

Hebrews 11:1

Romans 5:3-4

Psalms 119:114

Hebrews 10:23

Psalms 31:24

Romans 8:25

Micah 7:7

Psalms 25:5

Psalms 130:5

Psalm 33:22

Romans 5:5

1 Peter 1:3

Scriptures on Peace

Philippians 4:6-7

Psalms 4:8

Romans 8:6

1 Corinthians 14:33

Matthew 5:9

James 3:18

Romans 5:1-2

Job 22:21-22

John 14:27

Numbers 6:26

Isaiah 9:6

Proverbs 16:7

2 Thessalonians 3:16

Psalm 29:11

Psalm 37:11

2 John 1:3

Romans 12:17-18

Scriptures on Joy

Romans 12:12

Psalms 94:19

Habakkuk 3:18

Psalms 16:11

1 Peter 1:8–9

Isaiah 61:10

John 16:24

Proverbs 15:23

2 Corinthians 9:7

Romans 15:32

John 15:11

Psalm 119:111

Psalms 149:4

Psalms 119:14

Isaiah 55:12

Psalms 126:5-6

Scriptures on Salvation

John 3:16

Acts 4:12

Acts 16:31

2 Timothy 1:9

Psalms 62:1

Acts 2:21

Romans 10:10

Titus 2:11-12

Luke 19:10

2 Peter 3:9

Luke 18:27

Mark 16:16

Matthew 7:13-14

1 Peter 1:8–9

Hebrews 11:1

Hebrews 11:6

Romans 10:17

Dedication

This book is dedicated to all our family, friends, and everyone

we hold dear to our hearts.

But mostly, this book is dedicated to our Lord and Savior,

Jesus Christ.

About the Authors

Linda Diane Lay, Angelia Richhart, and Amber Richhart are poets, writers, and authors of multiple great books. They reside in Indiana and have a love for poetry and the arts. They have written an inspirational book named

"Divinely Guided," which surrounds and entails the subjects of faith, love, hope, peace, and joy. While this book offers an inspirational message of love and acceptance through Jesus Christ, this book is based on Christianity and love. It is a good read for anyone wanting to learn more about Christianity, deepen their faith, and strengthen their relationship with Christ.

They have also written three poetic books that are anthologies, which are collections of poems from each author compiled together in one beautiful work, such as "The Sugar Orchard," "The Essence of a Pearl," and "Poetic Colors." These books dive deep into the depths of femininity and the emotions that women feel throughout life. Such as love, joy, and bliss, as well as exploring the sad poetic symphonies of pain, grief, and loss. These three books have words that will touch your heart and soul, as well as words of wisdom, heartache, love, and grief that we have all felt throughout our lives. The words they use reflect such deep emotions that you will have cried the tears they've shed and shared the joy and feel as if you have encountered these life experiences yourself.

Linda Diane Lay, Angelia Richhart, and Amber Richhart use such passion and poetic expression when they write that the pages are engulfed in raw emotions. Anyone who reads their words from any of their poetic books can always relate to the emotions that they too have felt.